Forever and always,
for my two sons,
Adrian and Luca.

"Mom, do zebras think
they are really
handsome?"

I don't doubt it, Adrian.

"Mom, do you know what
a love cry is? When you
love someone so much,
you cry."

I love cry you everyday,
Luca (and you,
too, Adrian).

Text and Illustrations Copyright
© 2023 Jackie Adrian
First Edition. Brookeville, MD, USA
ISBN: 979-8-89034-003-0
Library of Congress Number: 2023908248

A Is for Alligator

...And Other Information to Entertain You

Jackie Adrian

A

is for Alligator

Meet Nelson. He likes to take morning jogs.
Did you know alligators can run?
Nelson is fast, but his brother is faster.

B

is for **Bird**

**Meet Wes. He likes to give compliments.
By the way, you are looking so lovely today.**

C

is for Cow

**Meet Celeste. She likes to speak in Spanish.
Hola, mis nuevas amigas! Te amare por siempre!**

D

is for Dinosaur

**Meet Clementine. She loves lolipops.
She usually brings several to share.
It would be easier if her tongue was longer.**

E

is for Egg

Inside is a baby goose.
Baby goose is dreaming about mac & cheese.
Someday, baby goose. Someday.

F

is for Flamingo

**Meet Ruby. They like to swim with crocs.
Nelson is their best friend.**

G

is for Gecko

Meet Edward. He likes to play tag.
It's hard to catch him when he climbs up walls!

is for Horse

Meet Sapphire. She is her own best friend.
She loves to draw, write stories,
and eat cherry pie.

is for Igloo

This igloo loves providing safety and warmth.
It also likes listening to the secrets
shared inside its walls.

J

is for Jellyfish

Meet Cece. She sometimes gets nervous. Water dancing always makes her more at ease.

K

is for Kelp

Kelp grow together to make kelp forests. Many
other sea creatures live in these forests, too.
Do you think they host under water parties?
I would go.

L

is for Lips

**Meet Fig. She loves to kiss.
Do you love to give or receive kisses?**

M

is for Mouse

Meet Paloma. She enjoys scavenger hunts.
Sometimes she hides her findings in
a small box.

N

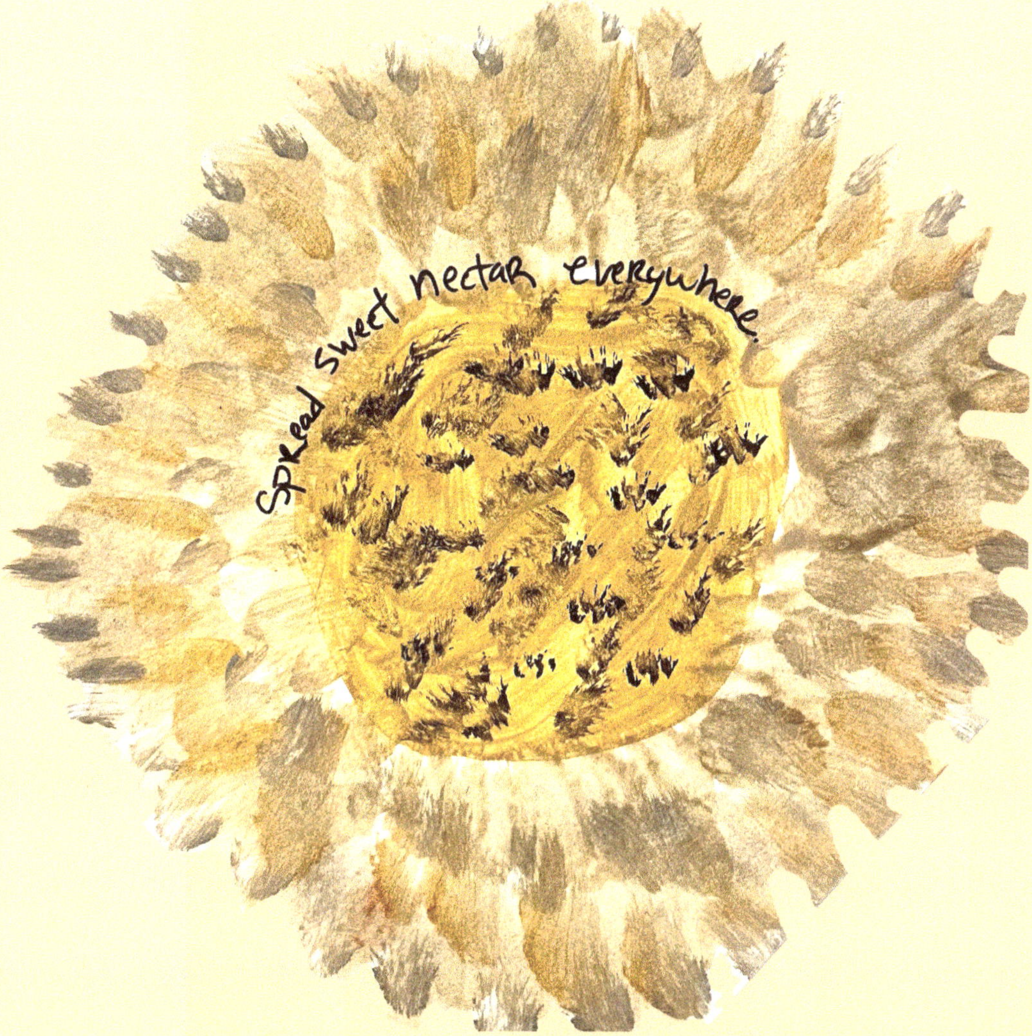

is for **Nectar**

Nectar provides sweetness and strength for whatever the day brings. Steal as much nectar as possible throughout your life.

O

is for Ostrich

Meet Barbara. They love to dress fancy.
The more sparkles, the better.

P

is for Panda

Meet Freddy. He likes to watch people and make up stories about what they might be thinking. He makes sure their thoughts are always nice things about him.

Q

is for Question

Questions are for everyone. Answered questions make us smarter, and sometimes calmer. Questions can also take away our worries. Questions are one of the best tools in life!

is for Road

Roads are for travelers. Some people are coming and some are going. Some travelers are happy and some are sad, but they all are going places. Where are you going?

S

is for Sunshine

Meet Vida. She knows how to warm us up, helpus grow, give us light, and make us happier just because she's here.

T

is for Toucan

Meet Ms. Pretty. She loves to sing in the trees and tell her friends they are spectacular.

U

is for Umbrella

Umbrellas protect us from wind, rain, and too much sunshine. Umbrellas can be spots of brightness on a dreary day.

V

is for Vulture

Meet Ari. Ari loves leftovers for every meal and is a surprisingly good sharer.

W

is for Whale

Meet Sebastian. He loves long vacations to
California where he eats his heart
out every year.

X

is for X-ray fish

Meet Lupita. She loves to learn and lets friends count her bones through her translucent skin during math class.

is for **Y**ak

Meet Jack. He likes to take evening strolls with his buddies. He sometimes has an attitude, but always knows when to apologize.

Z is for Zebra

Meet Angelica. She is proud of her unique stripes and personality. She is a great listener and tells silly jokes to her family.

cdefghijklmnopqrstuvwxyza
defghijklmnopqrstuvwxyzab
fghijklmabcdefghijklmnopqr
vwxyzabcdefghijklmnopqrs
vwxyzabcdefghijklmnopqrs
vwxyzabcdefghijklmnopqrs
vwxyzabcdefghijklmabcdef
ijklmnopqrstuvwxyzabcdef
ijklmnopqrstuvwxyzabcdef
jklmnopqrstuvwxyzabcdef
klmnopqrstuvwxyzabcdef
ijklmnopqrstuvwxyzabcdef
jklmabcdefghijklmnopqrst
vwxyzabcdefghijklmnopqrs
vwxyzabcdefghijklmnopqrs
vwxyzabcdefghijklmnopqrs
vwxyzabcdefghijklmabcdef
ijklmnopqrstuvwxyzabcdef
ijklmnopqrstuvwxyzabcdefghij